THE MOON CYCLE

i

EFFIE MIHOPOULOS

OMMATION PRESS 1991 CHICAGO

Offshoot Offset # 14
For subscribers to *Mati*, this is # 43/44

This project is partiallly supported by a grant from the City of Chicago Department of Cultural Affairs, and the Illinois Arts Council Access Program.

Some of these poems have previously been published or are about to appear in the following publications:

Attitude, A.U. Review, Bogg, Eulipian, Hammers, High Rock Review, Hob-Nob, Jazziminds Magazine, Minotaur, Mountain Moving, Orphic Lute, Poetalk, Poetry &, Poetry North Review, Riverrun, Sing Heavenly Muse!, Valley Women's Voice, Volume Number, Walking & Sinning, Wayward Wind and *Welter*.

ISBN 0-941240-17-7

Printed at Cosmos Press, Chicago

TABLE OF CONTENTS

TABLE OF CONTENTS

LOTUS

the moon is a wisp, a shadow.
you are indistinct, a blur.
you move so quickly into & out of my life,
you unbalance me with each facile phrase.
while I plod on with words as if I weren't a writer.
as if the moon weren't about to blossom
          so inevitably
          full.

MERCURY

the moon is like a shell
that breaks open tonight
                revealing you
                inside
                a pearl
the moon is like an oyster
an aphrodisiac tonight
as always
when we stare at it
white moon that shifts like an irritant
                travelling from day to night
                like an invisible messenger
                it sprouts wings
                in places where it shouldn't
                brings us news always
                that makes us
                breathe faster
how the moon breaks open tonight
like a walnut
ready to be consumed

I FLY ON WORDS TONIGHT

as I fly on words tonight,
my life exists without me, and I
pause:
      I peddle the moon
      tonight,
      sell words.
I listen to words tonight,
the moon's hungry aura around
me:
I spit the words out,
and the hollow moon that chases me:
      I whisper lies.

CAROUSEL

the stars are a buzz of sounds around me, how they whirl
like dancers. everything spins, excited: your eyes are twin
coals reflecting moonlight and serenades. blue is a touch
that whispers, yesterday was a long time ago. nothing could
conceivably be serene today, when the two of us blaze with
starlight. my hands are whorls of sound: how the air crackles
around us until we are browned and toasted like
marshmallows.

BLUEBLOOD IN REPOSE

the moon pumps in the sky
like your heartbeat
how you recline inside each star
odalisque in a bubble
odalisque in contrast
                white against dark
each minute is a marathon
till you draw closer
how you recline inside each sphere
                of light
odalisque in radiation
odalisque in blue
                blueblood
each minute is a sun
that keeps me burning
till you draw closer

CRESCENTS

they are everywhere
crescent-shaped moons that cradle me
          into dreams of dancing
          under a full moon
they leap out from your eyes into the air
          like dancers
          while the drums beat
          this is the chant
          watch how it works
see the gleam of metal in your eyes
reflected from my crescent-shaped jewelry
how we dance under the moonlight
only the gods between us

ATHLETES

there is a race we have not run yet, though we would both
like to whisper against the edge of a knife and see if it doesn't
cut. to shatter glass as if it weren't there.

watch the world disappear as I sit here beside you, perched
on a stool, ready for the aggressiveness of flight.

there is a traditional truce between enemies that follows as
naturally as the night does the day, and we are its imitators,
duplicates of such complex cycles as those of the moon's,
phases of the whole.

agile huntress and so fleet of foot, Diana the Moon Goddess
makes an impartial arbitrer, finds us equal adversaries,
judges us both on the verge of becoming victors.

WONDERLAND

the moon is a crescent shape overhead, a paper cut-out. abstract, geometric, distant and mechanical: the moon is something cool and unapproachable, a reigning queen disdainful of all others in her retinue. how she dazzles all those around her, resplendently, with all her jewels on parade. if only they were paste, so you could have a set made, too. bright red construction paper for rubies, blue for turquoise and sapphires, translucent white for pearls: what a splendid selection of diamond tiaras you could make. in the moonlight it almost looks real and oh so effective. count the sparkles in each eye regarding you, all the sparkling gems in each bright bracelet, set in each florid pin. how the moon dazzles you with its precision, a computer far away and above you, a condescending robot that never pauses to consult you for orders, but keeps proceeding ever onward endlessly, with nowhere real to go.

CLOWN FACE

the moon is sluggish tonight, dances like a clown shuffling his feet in a final desperate attempt to make the children around him laugh. the children stare, their eyes twin cookies made from the same mold, disapproving. he moves fast as he can, but never fast enough to please the children. they can't imagine being old, find it hard to believe he turns voluntarily like a penny turning on its axis about to stop, when all the time he could be spinning at full speed—fast—like a marble rolling over and over, getting places. he stays always in the same spot, stationary like the moon, always in the same position. this pirouette is slow, like the moon's progression from one phase to the next. the children can't know how easy it is to be tired at 25, 35 or 60.

the clown, on the contrary, can think only of this, as he brings first one foot up, then the other, jumps down onto both, that wide, tired grin on his face so exaggerated he knows the children will get the point, but they don't.

the moon wears whiteface like him, mimes its own demise, caresses the air like a hand drawing pictures. the door looks so real he almost steps through it into the next section of the dance, but catches himself the last minute. the children clap, they are convinced he has stopped breathing. there are only walls around him, he keeps pushing, but they won't move. the children push the air like he does, palms flattened, but they are ghosts. they pass through bricks as if they don't exist, they have a long way to go yet to reach the moon, to make it dance like a tired clown that can't stop crying.

REPEAT PERFORMANCE

moonrise
pebble

the earth distorts around me
like a snowflake looming into obscurity

cross-stroke

the earth breaks like a lake's surface
distorting like a million fragments
like my shattered   breathing

I hear your creak, footstep after
                              footstep
                              following
                              sleep
the lantern casts shadows
your body distorts
becomes a legion of different you's
                              extends
                              & breaks around me
                              into the same familiar
                              breathing patterns

PEGASUS

I live inside a box
                of answers
                open me
                nothing inside
                but the secrets of the moon
                        and how it moves
                        across the sky
                        like a chariot
                        without wheels
                        nothing inside
but the scorpion that hides
ready to strike
it lurks in a corner
under the lid
what a small price to pay
for knowledge
                        as you ride across the sky
                        your wings
                        on either side of you
                        like banners
                        in the wind
                        that blows you
                        always
                        in the direction
                        you want to go in

MOON PATTERNS

I

your harpoon's head jewelry
for ransom
the moon sits a prisoner

II

I look for you among the trees
I blunder, instead, into the moon

III

heirlooms of family tradition:
feather necklaces and crocheted
pearl brooches weigh
heavy on the sale of your
conscience
in the moonlight.

IV

Beethoven's stare is in the other room.
we look at the moon
instead.
avoiding that bronze, swollen gaze.
the moon is a metallic substitute.

V

the music we dance by
is contained by four walls,
the area of our disease

VI

faces spying on the moon
we broach the subject of
equality

VII

books bathed in moonlight
awaiting the dawn and the
garbage truck fervor

VIII

hot squalls of argument
we bend in the moonlit pattern
of faces

IX

the moon shatters your presence
lullabye of sound
we are dancing

X

the moonlight reaches silver hands
into the sound of your voice
my eyes are twin moons

AUCTIONEER

pearl-white,
the moon is a precious jewel.
sell it.
this night is worth a thousand necklaces
at whatever reckless auction you attend.
each brittle star in the audience
has its own garden of treasures.
measure yourself against it.
it is always the moon you lose yourself against
always the moon that emerges victorious from battle.
always the moon that goes to the highest bidder.

PIERROT'S REVENGE

for Kenneth Anger

the moon is transfixed tonight, garlands of roses
                              surround it.
a necklace around its neck, strands of lei
                              on either side of it,
two cherubs hold up
each side
for me to look at
a mirrored reflection
                              I look inside
                              it is you
the angels gaze at you fondly as they struggle
                              with their burden
as Atlas must have looked up at the sky
                              towards his gods
while the weight of the world kept getting heavier
                              and heavier
how readily he shifted it to the shoulders of another
how easy to trick someone that trusts you
the cherubs drop the load of the moon they carry
                              between them:

see how readily it shatters.

SHADOWBOXING

the moon casts blue shadows.
how they halo round each other
like children in the playground.
how the shadows become confused,
        falling one into the other
                            anklets on my feet
                            bangles on my arms
how the collar runs round your neck
like the shadows that circumference the moon
circling   circling   circling:

you are always closer than I think.

TRACER

17

the moon is a hollow ball:
follow it as it bounces
out of the universe,
away from you,
too far to retrieve.

WHISPERS

The moon is a monster,
a distant shadow.
It follows you everywhere,
dogs your footsteps
and keeps you a prisoner.
Quick, make a wish.
Blow out the birthday candles.
It just might go away,
like your lover.

TRAILING THE MOON

everything flies tonight
blue smoke and moonlight
everything flies like a kite
and we follow
          like children
          behind it

LIGHTWEIGHT BURDENS

the weight of the city crushes me like the weight of the
moon. how it threatens me, overhead, dangling like an
axe over my head, about to fall. how it reminds me of
you, casting the same shadow, a dancer's silhouette in
the air, about to land with a low thud on the stage. it
reminds me of an acrobat about to swing himself
through the air, up from his comfortable perch on the
chair, into the arms of a partner. it reminds me of the
trapeze artist going round and over the trampoline before
he steps off. there is no other way. your face is like the
moon's, pale, accusatory, always coming closer...

JUMPING

how far the moon is, such a distant toy. and how it
tempts you, sitting up there in the dark sky, to reach it.
it moves round you like a halo, a series of connected
patterns like a line of dancers, what fluid gracefulness as
it progresses through its phases, each classic variation
repeated ritually, month after month, the way you go
from day to day, resurrecting the same exercises at the
barre. you bend into the same routine you have been
trained in, obey those selfsame laws of etiquette you
have learned to abide by, which have become second
nature to you by now. *révérence.* the moon is as sacred
as your ballet teacher, commands respect. *révérence.*
bow to your teacher at the end of class. the teacher
bows back to you. it's the rules of the game, tradition
that no one wavers from. no one good, at least.

how you would love to see the moon give you applause
the way others round you do! one palm flat against the
other for approval, then clasped one round the other as
the beat gets more rhythmic and they demand you back.
how lovely to be in the spotlight, how natural, the
hospital is far away, the nurses are alien creatures: the
doctors mean only more tickets sold in the audience,
their salaries enough to fill the house. one dead seat
less. *jeté, jeté, jeté,* you circle like a panther, each leap
so dynamic the stage is too small to confine you, a cage
you want to break out of. *jeté, jeté, jeté,* you jump
higher, closer and closer to that moon that surrounds
you.

you long so much to touch it that you do, as I watch
from the shadows, a dark figure in silhouette, rapt at the
accolades of attention you acknowledge in the limelight,
a dancer, as you should be, walking the air as if it were
water, treading less carefully than you do at the barre,
away from home.

NEW PORTRAIT

the moon is a handle
crank it
see the motor begin to rev up
the big black void out there
expanding
see it protest
see it sputter & fume
                while it starts:
the moon is a handle
use it
see how the rocket
                takes us
where we have never gone before

FLASHES

my heart pierces shadows,
as the moon cools,
                breaks in half
                & goes nowhere.
(my heart in his eyes, shining)
the mechanics of skin
(my heart in his hair, yellow sun
that cracks: sunspots like
imperfections, in the air,
unlike his eyes.)
my mouth moves & the white moon
shines there.
                I see shadows
                crawl, from beneath his eyes,
                out from the corners:
& the moon is his flaming face,
his eyes, the horizon, an even blue
without sunspots:
I watch his mouth move
like his eyes
                against me.

FAVORITES: RANK AND FILE

the moon is a howler tonight, full & passionate. you, as always, are easily embraced. the moon is a cry in the night, implacable, white heat against all Greek tradition. you are white lightening, flashy smiles. you watch the fire-filled sky, ablaze with dawn. you and the day are the same canvas gone wild with color, Turner times Gauguin, everything tonight is my favorite, you and the moon, everything becomes a crazed matchmaker. a crazy matched pair, haunting me with the sounds of the night multiplying until the dusk brings liberation with a resplendent palette, bronzed for posterity. you want to make this moment tonight special, as if it supercedes every other, as if this howling moon were any more noteworthy than any other.

but it is the same full moon we witness regularly, no different than it usually is for us, shining with the same intensity, bright, cathartic. you and the moon and the darkening day have always been my irreplacable favorites, why should tonight be any different, why worry about commemorations?

the moon is always ablaze with passion overhead, and the sun is always ushered into and out of the sky with the pomp and circumstance of color that is its due. the moon is a howler tonight, as it is once a month, dependable as always: I can count on it as much as you, inevitably there to please, twin bookends. and I have always been addicted to reading.

WATCHING THE MOON

the moon begins to break
                and scatter
                like a jigsaw puzzle
                it circles round me
                like an asteroid belt
                each piece is a problem
                I cannot solve
I have always wanted
                to shrink into an atom
                to have electrons & neutrons
                        surround me
                        like a crowd
                each orbit is a prison
                I cannot escape
the moon begins to strangle me
it is never appeased
                no matter how much
                I grow
                to resemble it
                no matter how I disintegrate
                no matter how many pieces
                I break into
                to please it
        the moon & I
                are like twins
                no matter what we do
                no matter how much momentum
                we gather
                the force of gravity holds us
                close to home

                    like the leash on a dog
                    rattle the chains all you want
                    if you stretch too much
                    the collar will choke you
I have always wanted to be a skeleton
                              my bones rattling
                              who was it
                              scattered bones
                              like seeds
and had the earth crawling with soldiers
throw mine around
                         to cast a spell
                         to predict the future
                         the omens are bad
throw the dog a bone
how the earth will crawl with poets
how they will all look at the moon
                              bone-white
                              and think
                              only
                              of castanets
                              ole ole
the moon is a gypsy thinking of the future
a flamenco dancer inspired by
                    the flames of prediction

ATLANTIS

the weight of the city oppresses me, builds and builds on my shoulders till it is unbearable. it grows like a *papier maché* globe, one more layer of paper or kleenex making it fatter and bigger, more of a burden to carry. it'll never dry. the weight of the city holds me captive the way gravity pulls the Earth in toward the Sun, will never let it escape—the way the Earth holds the Moon, dead and darkened, but still a precious prisoner by its very presence alone, something to lend the planet importance. one prisoner is better than none. how can I escape, my bulk only an ant compared to the planets, or maybe even smaller, who knows. a mathematician I'm not, let them build all those models, comparing Earth—Moon—Sun to scale, how would I know the exact figures, and what do they matter?

all I know is that I'm nothing compared to any of them, and there are chains that they cannot break, so how can I conceivably break mine? all I do is circle faster, like a top instead of a slow Christmas display, whirl and whirl like a dervish until I explode into a thousand poems. they trail like rose petals behind me, the fragments of a planet, like the asteroid belt. see what fighting back has done for me, broken me into a thousand fragments. see if you can count them. of course you can't. there are too many of them. most of those bits of rock circling the sun are nameless, too many of them to keep track of, worthless.

now a planet, on the other hand, is a thing to reckon with, like a city. like a basket of flowers full to the brim: everybody wants it. no one looks at you when the basket is empty. what a burden to carry, a basket of poems. the city weighs on me, always dull as its inhabitants on holidays, dim-witted on other days, how the city preys on me like a vampire. the city feeds on blood, fresh poet's blood—red roses, I give you three. count the suicides. one for the captor, one for the victim, one for the Moon. count your heart beating and beating under its burden of flesh, *1-2-3, 1-2-3.* how the city weighs on you, walls coming at you from all sides, squeezes you like a gorilla too happy to see its young. *1-2-3, 1-2-3.* what a lovely melody this waltz makes, my dear. would you care for the next dance? the city houses you, an able partner. there are balls everywhere, with couples dancing. dressed up in their finest. they are waiting for the music to stop, so they can rest. they are waiting for the music to stop so they can leave their partner. they are waiting for the music to stop so they can go home, bored as they arrived. *1-2-3,* what a lovely refrain. the weight of the city stifles me, the air reeks with it, heavy with gravity as usual, pulling me and everything else where it doesn't want to go.

I FIND SHELTER

I'm going now   he says
and I scrape my knee against the desk
          (the pain, the pain of it all
          like vaccinations)
and he comes to visit me later
but by this time it doesn't matter anymore
          (it's not true
          that it's never too late
          some things *age*)
and from outside, the Chicago winter enters
he brings it in, cold as his eyes
not even his dark beard brings his face into focus
not even the dark moustache against his pale face
and when he talks about harvest
          his eyes focus
          like the apex of a pin
          like a weapon
but I am immune by now
and he doesn't bring the moon any closer

DISTANCES

the moon feasts on stars tonight
as I watch it
digests them like an overfed cat
chokes
spits them out like olive pits
bullets that cause new wounds
the moon stops moving tonight
doesn't even whirl itself into circles
like a mad dog twirling round and round

in your absence
it stops telling me the secrets
it has always revealed,
giving me mandates like Pythea
about where and how you were
the moon stops tracing the circumference of stars,
winding its way between them
like a runner in an obstacle course
stands, instead, like a statue,
tired, even, of the least exertion.
stock-still
I contemplate it
the way we used to do
together
it shines like it always has
a pale, cold color
as if nothing has changed
as if you were still wide-eyed
under its halo
I stare at it

an accomplice without a partner
blink once
see how it dissolves
blink twice
see how your image fades also
how the moon continues to shine tonight
for everyone else
like a magic lantern
the light cutting a clear, straight line
to everything they have always wanted

but concerning you and me
the moon stops moving tonight
doesn't dance as it always has
around us.
at the most,
it makes only false starts—
until it stops completely,
a tether ball with no one to set it into motion
crowding the sky as you crowd my memory

the moon goes against the grain tonight
doesn't follow its regular patterns
beats its path against my pulse:
instead of giving me violin accompaniment
I hear only percussion
without you here to conduct it all
everything falls apart
breaks into a thousand stars
even the moon pauses to rest tonight
trying to find you
and bring you back

CAT'S CRADLE

you caress the night with your unlikely letters,
making the moon intense for me,
making it a strong and wonderful perfume
that fills the room.
broken hearts are far away
yet
today I see only love in front of me
and your words make the night still glitter
more than the Christmas card I taped to the wall
yesterday
underneath all the flashing lights
such a smile you have
that breaks quickly across your face
flashes on and off like the lights
I watch
waiting for it
like blinking Christmas lights in windows.
there has always been a part of me that loved
gaudy things.
why should I disregard you?
vowel after vowel
the words become syllables,
a steady stare.
it seems difficult to believe that you are so far away
today
when I need you most.
I write back that I see you stand inside my house,
more real than all your letters.
who am I to believe
the flagrant moon overhead
or your letter?

it has always been difficult for me to decide.
I always wanted everything, all the choices.
so people wind up giving me
more than they ever intended
and I reciprocate
until
we find ourselves embroiled in a thick paste
of affection
suddenly this letter is meaningless to me
without you here.
I don't want to reply, want only
to throw it away.
what can I say about this moment
and the previous one
and the one I am about to feel?
what can I say to cross the gulf between us?
distance is such an unlikely concept to me.
separation and time have always been equally
incomprehensible.
I could never figure them out.
how can you be talking so pleasantly to someone
one minute
and the next
you know you'll never see them again.
the next thing you know, you don't know.
how can I make it make sense to you
if I don't understand it either?
at all, in fact.
send me another letter.

maybe I'll have it all solved by then.
maybe I'll be working on a psychological novel
like Pushkin
that I'll abandon without compunction because
I got what I needed from it
or found out that I never would.
or maybe I'll just still be staring at the moon
for answers that never seem to come,
that never seem to fit our situation,
so much more complex than it seemed at first.
only a few months' separation—always the unexpected,
or the likelihood of things to happen that you try
to forget.
like writing a poem, that first minute of inspiration
makes you forget about all the revisions
you have to go through before you are satisfied.
you try not to think about all the hard work
behind your craft,
the way you try to forget about compromises.
I have nothing to say in response to your florid,
romantic words.
they fill the night with such ease.
now it is harder for me to write back, to be so
confident.
it never occurs to me that things can be righted
once they have gone wrong.
once someone dies, you can't resurrect them,
unless you're Lazarus.
and how many of them have there been around.

ADOLESCENCE

the flamboyance of the moon dancing outside annoys us. how dare it sit out there, pretending it is pedigreed when we know damn well all it can do is barely stutter a quick howdedo before it tries its pirouette and falls flat on its face, leaving us a mass of tangled laughs, trying not to expose our tired approval of its fallen grace, trying to make ourselves look like total strangers.

you nod your head, I acquiesce. we pretend not to know any answers, though long ago we gave up our positions as nominated judges. brace yourself for this one. they think we are speaking in code, forgetting that long ago the moon gave up all its secrets to us, spilling them out the way you pour sugar into a bowl. the moon never knew how to dance well, gets by on half-truths—knows it only too well—and basks in our knowledge of its ignorance. but this audience, watching it and applauding, doesn't. and the moon smirks out at us, half-amused with itself, as we are. we have been partners for years, bored by it all, by each other—but everyone else bores us even more. so we stay together. the moon refreshes us periodically. the moon and its jesting clown self, dancing always to that same tune through the ages, the same predictable routine we have come to expect, attached to it as much as children to a fairytale.

if the moon danced well tonight, I think we would be so shocked we'd keel over. a fine hoopla you have gotten us into tonight, the moon ignoring its darker side in honor of this laughing, merry self, so unlike us. tonight the moon is slumming, or pretends to, though it dances maliciously sweet in its natural environment. the band begins to play, you ask me for the pleasure of this next dance. what a farce. we are as oppressed as always, as opposed and as similar as two pebbles on the beach. you can't tell one from the other. shall we dance, shall we imitate the moon? the trouble is to extricate ourselves from this complicated mass of laughter where we have buried ourselves, the tattooing going in further than skin deep. I can't think of a single reason why not, so we might as well dance while the moon is still a sliver, otherwise it might make a bigger *faux pas*, and we'll never manage to stop laughing long enough.

ON THE SUBJECT OF INTERVIEWS

you sit inside the moon
like a racer inside a car:
          does your face get dirty
          under your visor
          when you drive too fast?
          do the muscles in your arms tense
          till you can't move?
          do you think of trophies
          often
          or not at all?
have you ever consiered falling asleep
          till your eyes turn silver
          like the moon's?
will you pose for Whistler's *Portrait of the Artist's Moon*?
will you recognize yourself
when you look inside the mirror?
will you think of me
and how I love to touch silver?

how you sit inside the moon like Rip van Winkle:
does your beard tickle you?
would you like to shave it off?
do you talk like him in a language
that no one understands?
count the syllables in iambic pentameter
and what do you get?
the number of times a "t" repeats itself
or the number of times the moon yawns,
bored with itself?

how you sit inside the moon like an overfed cat:
did you eat too many fish today?
                count them.
did you drink too much milk, or only water?
                measure it.
have you ever cooked your own meal?
have you ever addressed yourself a memo?
did you ever take sleeping pills when you were a child?

how you sit inside the moon like a picture inside a
frame:
it has always been your most evident secret
that you have always wanted to be a poet
                just like the moon.

AND NOW BEETHOVEN

There are trees across the river on the embankment. Follow them with your eyes like a travelogue to your destination. Blink twice when you get there. Count the number of times you have been betrayed. Multiply by six. Divide your answer by the number of times you have seen the moon dance on stilts. Think of yourself as you were at the party, dancing and drinking, think of what you were wearing. Subdivide if you wish by the number of parties you have been to this week, last week, and the week before. How much time was wasted? How much time will it take you to calculate the answer? Everything is optional at affairs like these, black tie and all. Count the number of times you have seen the sky turn somersaults in its sleep like an acrobat, backwards. How many times have you seen these trees bend back as if they were in conference about you? Conspiracy is in the air. Listen to the music that comes from the other side of the river, compliments of the breeze. It is in deference to you that they are playing Beethoven. Bend your neck a little over to the right. Just the composition the artist wanted. As you listen, neck craned forward, think of how you almost jumped through this very window. How many times? Was it in this lifetime or the last? Was it in this dimension or the next? Was it in this house or some other?

Think instead of the moon staring back at you overhead, while the artist paints. Give him time to finish his picture. There will be other rivers in your life, other trees.And that same moon overhead, dangling. $37 \times 6 = 10$ and something. In a minute, you can compute the rest. $45 \times 53 \times \pi =$ another. Add to it the number of concerts you have heard with Beethoven's music. Subdivide by addition or subtraction the number of lives you have changed, the number of faces you have borrowed. Don't give me the answer. Keep the tally all to yourself.

ST. VITUS' DANCE: JUDI'S STORY

for Judi Baba

I wear the halo of disguise
the frugality of fireworks explodes around me
like a warm coat, the security of children
weaving itself into a kaleidoscopic veil
before my eyes, broken windows, gaping from
          the center of their dark rings
          and yet each night I dance
          naked to the moon
          like a skeleton among shadows,
          God's blinking Sears eye
          blesses me and sanctifies our matrimony
he is not a jealous lover the way you are
but winks blindly in the daylight
when I clean the house, cook for you
and sleep beside you like a soot-soaked Cinderella
till the midnight hour strikes
          and then I rise to keep my rendezvous,
          to dance the night away without you
the landscape of my body becomes a celebration
          of fireworks, discharging colors
          into the eye of the night,
          my secret lover

SHOUTING

your name whirls
like a merry-go-round
        inside me
whirls and gathers momentum
        like a dervish forbidden by law to dance
        I think of you when I shouldn't
your face flashes before me like an icon,
your name affixed at the bottom,
like an artist's signature.
I repeat your name like a talisman.
I carry it inside me like the magic bundle
        my mother pinned inside my dress
        to protect me against the Evil Eye
how your eyes are different
how they share their glance with the moon
how they dazzle me with their color.
I think of you each time I hide inside the forest
        when my life becomes a puzzle
        when each tree becomes a shadow
        when each shadow becomes a statue
        that threatens me,
        when each statue becomes a stranger:
I think of you and your name becomes an emblem
        that protects me.
how everything beeches against you
        like waves against sand
you become an anchor
and everything comes to port against you

your name is like a magic number
that everyone calls on more than once
I cross my fingers like a child and make a wish
        you are suddenly real again
        filling me with such happiness
        that I long to burst like a bubble
and how I want everything else to break too

WATCHING THE MOON GROW

I

its cycle
casts such shadows
around your eyes

II

the days lapse into nights,
break like waves against minutes
that line the shore of the room:
froth over froth
over thick wet sand.
we turn our lives into blankets.

III

the moon begs to increase itself,
bleats like a lamb.
like a baby in a womb it grows to twice
then three times its original size,
grows into a fat infantile-smiled roundness:
one big full face that blinks and blinks
as if it were winking,
and burps back the excess milk.
your days regurgitate also.

IV

the moon, once a tiny wisp of a thing,
becomes a full-fledged musketeer,
the size of an unforgivable tumor.
bloated with restraint, it knows, too,
like a new-age medic, how to heal itself.
the moon knows about conversions, revisions
and instantaneous re-write.
it has always had computers for lovers.
the moon knows how to go
from the unwanted disease of largesse
to a lessened self
the lesser of two evils
the moon knows how to cut itself in two,
halves itself regularly in its monthly cycle,
becomes with each passing day
another version of a sliver.
another version of what it is and isn't,
and what it can be.
the moon becomes an image
any image
whatever you want it to be:
all images, and none.
watch the moon blow out its gills like a fish,
in and out,
until it becomes more alien than you ever imagined,
its gibbous impact a cocktail sneer
you can't help imbibing.

THE MOON OVERHEAD

the distance between you and the moon is a shadow you
follow like tracks across the snow. you follow it compulsively,
not knowing what you are doing and not particularly caring,
either. you don't know why you like ice cream or opera or
blond, blue-eyed men, but you do. and that's that. so the
moon is a trail that echoes you, footsteps resounding against
a hard wood floor, the kind that always make you want to
know where the person is going. it must be toward something
important, somewhere interesting. things shrouded in
mystery are always more exciting. that's what my teachers
taught me, my college professors who read poems and wrote
them themselves, the ones who should know. the great
unknown is always more enticing than the predictable, and
the moon is the biggest puzzle of all, that no one has solved.
it turns poets into pests, detectives who want to know
everything—what it's all about—makes them persistent as
spies. working without orders, on their own missions, poets
with too many words, or not enough.

you can never quite find the right ones, those special sacred words, and how the air aches around you because of it. your head becomes a puzzle, too, though nothing new gets resolved because of it. yet you feel pleased somehow, at the same old discoveries, and that's better than nothing, I suppose. whether you learn something new or not, the moon also repeats itself, one phase after another, what distorted forms it takes on. the same odd shapes. how beautiful the moon is some days when it changes, though it is always the same moon shining overhead, that you always recognize, whether you like it or not, whether you look for it consciously or notice it haphazardly here and there: on a walk, going out to buy groceries, coming back from the ballet. it is that same moon that follows you overhead, like a shadow of itself, the real one.

HOSPITALS

how the moon is like the sun
        both of them circles
        both of them stars
        both of them a reflection
            of your many faces
how you multiply yourself into sunspots
how you divide yourself into phases of the moon
        disguise yourself for the crowd
            into loaves and fishes
oh how you abound like the remnants
            of a broken mirror
        each of them is a curse
        a miscalculation
        a cancerous cell
watch them divide and multiply with all that
            modern technology
you grow into a thousand patients
        each of them craves a cure
        each of them clutches you like a cane
        each of them confronts Death and turns it
            into a Savior
how the doctors look at you as if you were special
and the nurses pamper you
as if you were writing a book about all of them
how the hospital reminds you of the moon
its whiteness everywhere reflected,
sheets inside a washing machine,
spinning behind the glass:
you long to shatter it into a thousand bullets
you long to name each one as if they were your children
each one of them, living on the moon,

                permanent inhabitants
how you would like to think of them gazing at the sun
                the way you look up
                at these white hospital lights
                so bright, so intense
you scatter yourself about the room
                each piece of you is a potsherd
                from an ancient vase
you wait for some dedicated archeologist
                to piece it all together correctly
                to make you whole
how you would like to be in a thousand places at once
                one of you a sign above his door
                one of you a paperweight in his office
                one of you the writing tools on his desk
how you would like to be the article he is working on
and the subject of his conversation
                the one he always thinks about
you wait patiently for him to add you to his collection
                of prized possessions
                becoming in the process
another broken vase on the floor
that he knocks over absent-mindedly
when he moves his hand in the wrong direction
one more broken vase
among a thousand others across so many other rooms
so many other hospitals
so many doctors
you wait, shattering yourself so deliberately

waiting
watching
waiting
how you are like the sun and the moon now
both of them at once
a wasteland
both of them
extreme
both of them devoid of alien life
empty vases full of nothing but hollow air
nothing to hide inside themselves
no kind of vegetation
how you have always hated the color green
and never quite
knew
why

PAS DE DEUX

seaweed gathers
in the air
between us
spins on its
ambiguous legs
into pirouettes
turns ambitious
cartwheels
circling
always closer
twining round
your neck first
then mine
until we are both
drowned under
the weight of our
separations, gasping
for the air
already occupied
by seaweed.

PAS DE DEUX II

for Norman McLaren

she moves, sinuously
arms swaying
circle swans:
  she moves abruptly, bends
  back: curvature,
  extension
  point:
  she "kicks"
  while she poses: the mechanics
of television, two
dancers from one
  on the floor,
  she becomes a bundle of
  movement:
the etiquette of dancers,
synthesis of curves:
dancers on stage, mirror reflections:
she hugs to herself, as the man approaches:
the mood of implication
  flutes, pipes,
  in Greek we call it
  φλογέρα
  the shepherd's pastoral:
  the combination of stance—
  hands, feet: extended:
  man, woman become
  triangle:
  surrounded in the glow of
  their own images, he leaves,

then multiplies, each in their own individuality
                    of movement, they
                    integrate
                    he reappears
                    to affirm her dancing
                    to watch and
                    to hold her,
                    waist-wise
                    taking positions
                    to her
                    like children,
while she moves in refractions
of light:
                    like snow, like rain
                    vari-colored, hands twirl:
the magician's hand, technician
making love to movement
                    mandala, lotus
                    hands ascend
                    contraction—release
I can almost hear Martha's voice &
                    from the floor, he raises her high,
                    blending:
                    his arms, his legs
                    her arms, her legs:
                    all reflections of images that travel in
                    slow motion,

                    into the mountains
                    into the lily-white dance-wing,
                    angel of tuffeta & tulle
                    that is absent, but in the angle of the
eye, as it disappears
the peacock is present:
                                preening in camera-wise
                                illusion, the surreal element
                                of voice, summing up
the dream they play on us, these dancers:
white snow on the television, the veil of hands,
                    falling in millions of tones of white and
                    white,
ruling my head &
my heart at the same time:
description of the pause,
the words before the end
                                connecting sun & sunshine
                                dance & dancer
                                connecting
                                what we love
to ourselves:
a sea of arms, & movement
waves

PAS DE DEUX III

your ghost follows me everywhere,
waddling like the moon behind me,
self-consciously.
your ghost follows me doggedly,
ignoring the weather,
the people around me,
the moon trembling overhead.
your ghost trails me despite everything,
taking each step with me,
breathing each breath.
the air becomes a leash that binds us
closer and closer
until
I am as much
your shadow
as you are

PAS DE DEUX IV

Galileo thinks of himself as a scale:
in either hand I hold the balance of my life.
on this side the truth, on the other side survival,
this leg represents the right step,
the other leg a false interpretation.
on the left side is a string
        that they pull to make me a puppet
on the right side is another
        that I snip myself
there is only one way to dance
        so convincingly
        that the audience begins to doubt
        you are not that same person on the stage,
        a real-life character,
        and I do it:
        I deny the world is round
        (such a blasphemy, my slow pavane),
        and yet it moves.

PAS DE DEUX V

I. *Swan Lake*

Picture this set:
Midnight sky.
The moon seems to be pirouetting across it,
just for this ballet.
The moon is a ballerina on parade.
In a white tutu, the same disguise as the moon.
She always was a traditionalist at heart.
This could only be a *ballet blanc.*
The diamonds on her bodice flash
as if about to pierce the night with Cupid's arrows.
A little mythology in the ballet.
After all, it started that way
depicting gods among mortals.
She looks around her
Everything pales next to the glaring pools of his eyes.
Only he can rescue her, the eternal lover.
The moon is a *danseur noble* now,
                    black tights, tight vest.
Everything is a dark velvet backdrop.

Okay, now here's the conflict to add some plot
to this series of *divertissements*: she's under a spell.
She and her friends can only be white swans
                    until they are free
and that other Evil One knows her disguise,
knows how to dress exactly like her,
how to become Odette's shadow.

Odile wears a black tutu
wanting to be thin and entice the Prince,
to take him away, confuse him.
Odette's snow white hands begin to thicken with down
when she feels betrayal,
begin to glisten silver feathers.
No matter what she does, it's wrong,
and he makes the guilt that rides the night air
                        like a witch
                        mount even higher.
He thinks the other is her,
pledges his love to the double.
Who knows, maybe he was only pretending
he couldn't tell the difference.
Men never realize the consequences of their actions
until it's too late.
She's forever a swan again, and no salvation.
Goodnight sweet prince.
The moon does *piqué* turns, its leg extending each time
                        to the side, pointing, accusing.
O evil magician, free her from this curse right now.
Like *chaîné* turns, one mistake linked to another,
a medallion around her neck,
the moon becomes a pendant.

II. *Giselle*

Picture this set:
Happy peasants dancing everywhere.
Everything starts out bright sunshine,
but, of course, things will change.

Contrast. Drama. Conflict.
The ballerina is a bright yellow sun that
melts into a slow, maddened death. Betrayed.
End of Act I. She's a ghost in the second.
She's under a big pale moon once again.
This is the crux of the ballet.
Her lover is a dancing fever. He must dance to live,
                    till sunrise.
If he drops, he dies. The Wili ghosts will have him.
She fights to let him live, keeps partnering him.
He does, and leaves her once again,
among the undead.
The ballerina is tired of all these death scenes.
She imagines the plot
going forward beyond the traditional point:
two night later
when her lover is gone and Giselle has only Hilarion
                    for company
                    her designated *fiancé*, The Hunter,
when it seems that she has only
the trembling moon overhead for lonely company
and it becomes a pale lantern that guides her
into a raucous nightly revenge
the rest of her days, when she knows how to hate,
one wild-eyed Wili among so many vengeful others
she never cried for Hilarion as she is doing now
                    for Albrecht

it's the nature of tragedy
to be a dancer that knows how to act out
a melancholy shiver of guilt
locked against moonlight
that never lets you break
completely free.

BLUE MOONLIGHT

I look from moon to lake tonight
and note how your eyes reflect them both
your eyes glide across the surface of my skin like swans
wrap themselves around me like eels
they swim like sapphires under water
                    pools of movement
I float against your breath like a boat on the river
your body is a dancer's, turning, always faster
like the spokes of a wheel
                blue moonlight breaks against the bushes
                blue moonlight hides behind the trees
                blue moonlight takes me traveling
like you, always further
      blue carnations
      blue roses
      blue hair
how your eyes resemble music tonight
      each note parades into another
      each glance becomes the next invitation to dance
      each second becomes another carnival time
                at the river
I would like to dress like a ghost for you
I would like to shrink to the size of a miniature
I would like to dance inside the circle of your eyes
      tracing their gaze, miming the ballet,
      that landscape that your eyes follow
how we resemble characters in a fairytale
and the moon dances overhead like Pavlova tonight

its white face resembles a crown
how you stand next to me like a marble statue
    your eyes only on me, like the eyes of a tomcat
I am lost beside you the way a mouse is magnetized
how you turn my mind into a marionette
    you make me purr like your feline mate
    and I am lost beside you
you depend on these manipulations
    the way a miner does on his pick
you depend on excavation tonight
the way a dancer does on a daily barre
you depend the same way for me to lean on you,
    waiting to be partnered
you depend on me the way a blind man does on his dog,
    on his red-tipped white cane
how you control me like a puppet and
your hands are the strings tonight
and they tremble while you work on me
they resemble a pair of dice, falling randomly
    wherever
    everywhere
your hands have muscles like a dancer's
    hardened into rock
my skin is rough diamonds that you smoothe into glass
    a plate window pane
I serve you apprentice-like
I spoil you like an only child
I sashay across the stage of your eyes like a siren

how you have always wanted to bend like a dancer
to close your eyes just once and forget to open them
I float against your breath like Ophelia
> *blue daisies*
> *blue fennel*
> *blue columbines*

how I have always thought of harlequins and pierrots as
dancers, such tragic figures under Picasso's
blue paintbrush, under his blue moonlight stare
but they have always been only clowns for you
> *blue violets*
> *rosemary*
> *and rue*
> *some for me*
> *and some for you*

I have always found it difficult to remember
where one thing stops and another starts
regret is like a round egg
everything inside the sphere moves
which came first, love or hunger
yours or mine
the chicken or the egg
which came first
regret, remembrance or the circle
there is never any escape from blue water,
from the river contracting
under the moon's blue shadows
blue moonlight travels across my shoulders
blue moonlight hides under my neck
blue moonlight breaks my bones as if they were candy

how easy it is to cap the jar
once the insect is caught inside
how easy it is to lure me, your eyes a lair
once the spider sets its trap,
the insect is so easily netted
and I am tangled inside the web of your eyes
I dance the tarantella tonight only for you
                pansies are blue
                parrots are too
                and
blue moonlight hides under my eyelids
blue moonlight breaks under my breasts
blue moonlight takes me from your eyes
                to your heartbeat
how I repeat myself, following close behind you
                a tight tango
your eyes circle me like prey, leap like tigers
they step inside me the way spirits do through walls
                and take possession
you play the role of the creditor who takes everything
in full stride, everything has changed hands until
we are only a tangle of limbs and everything dissolves
                in the blueness of air tonight
how quickly the lake and the moonlight
                become blue embers
                your eyes become empty swimming pools
                like mine
and your arms relax around me until they drop
                like overripe fruit
                figs from a tree

and how I long for that favorite taste against my tongue
                    tonight as always
the moon is like a big blue star in a coloring book
                    of planets
how we reach for it eager as children
how transparent the sky is
like the lake, your eyes, my mouth breathing warm air
how we long for blue moonlight to taste,
for blue moonlight to cover us, midsummer shroud,
till blue gauze wakes us
you tie my hair into blue strings
it takes us longer to recover,
                    like dancers past their prime
                    how they look at each other,
the studio walls around them covered with mirrors
they remember skating on the glass lake
how the audience was so convinced it was real
the mirror was their only secret
how your eyes reflect me
how my eyes resemble yours
the moon and the lake are like shadows
                    that crawl closer
they make us writhe and the audience is convinced
                    that nothing binds us
how only we know that all chains are real
and some tighter than others
the moon and the lake are like sailors tonight
                    always navigating closer
how quickly we resemble a shipwreck after the storm
how quickly we break apart like the rigging of a ship

we learn to leave each other like migratory birds
that move on toward home after they rest
                        another home
the moon disappears quickly from the surface of the lake
blue moonlight becomes dark shadows
your eyes reflect black moons, my eyes are mirrors
                        draped black for mourning
I am a weeping willow, a widow in black veils
how quickly we voluntarily become strangers once again
how quickly we part
like the moon and the lake when they separate
                for the day
                the dawn's splash of color
                so much like sunset
you can't tell them apart in photos unless you know
who took the picture and when
there is a touch of blue moonlight behind the edges
                of both
                your eyes are like the lake
                your eyes are like the moon
                your eyes are a sepia photograph
that we always become under the phases of the moon
                that turn us into vines
                twin reflectors twined
as if we were in a black and white photograph
                hand-colored by an artist
                who is obsessed by blue
                and moonlight
                equally

DISAPPEARANCES

68

I am at war with the moon tonight
I march forward on it
      till it shatters
I am at war with the moon
with the empty space that
      it used to occupy
how I hate everything about it
      even
the void it leaves behind
just think of it:
only the blind sky there
where the moon once stood
      dancing